Odd Blocks

CW00544638

Kay Ryan was born in California
County, California, since 1971. She has received numerous
awards for her poetry, including the Pulitzer Prize, the Ruth
Lilly Poetry Prize, fellowships from both the Guggenheim
Foundation and the National Endowment for the Arts, and
the Ingram Merrill Award. She has been a Chancellor of the
Academy of American Poets since 2006, and was the sixteenth
United States Poet Laureate from 2008 to 2010.

SR
E2.99
6A/39

KAY RYAN

Odd Blocks

Selected and New Poems

CARCANET

First published in Great Britain in 2011 by
Carcanet Press Limited
Alliance House
Cross Street
Manchester M2 7AQ

Poems from *Elephant Rocks*, *Say Uncle*, *The Niagara River* and the new
poems 'Odd Blocks', 'The Edges of Time', 'Bait Goat', 'Train-Track
Figure', 'Virga', 'Dogleg', 'Ledge', 'The Pharaohs', 'Pentimenti', 'Bitter
Pill', 'Finish', 'Easter Island', 'Spiderweb' and 'Still Life with Lemons,
Oranges and a Rose' from *The Best of It: New and Selected Poems*,
published in the United States in 2010 by Grove Press, an imprint of
Grove / Atlantic, Inc., 841 Broadway, New York, NY 10003, USA.
Poems from *Flamingo Watching* were first published in the United States in
1994 by Copper Beech Press, POB 2578, Providence, RI 02906, USA.
Poems and selection copyright © Kay Ryan 2011

The right of Kay Ryan to be identified as the author of this work
has been asserted by her in accordance with the
Copyright, Designs and Patents Act of 1988

All rights reserved

A CIP catalogue record for this book is available from
the British Library
ISBN 978 1 84777 130 8

The publisher acknowledges financial assistance from Arts Council England

Supported by
ARTS COUNCIL
ENGLAND

Typeset by XL Publishing Services, Tiverton
Printed and bound in England by SRP Ltd, Exeter

For Carol Adair
1942–2009

CONTENTS

Odd Blocks

from *Flamingo Watching* (1994)

FLAMINGO WATCHING

Wherever the flamingo goes,
she brings a city's worth
of furbelows. She seems
unnatural by nature—
too vivid and peculiar
a structure to be pretty,
and flexible to the point
of oddity. Perched on
those legs, anything she does
seems like an act. Descending
on her egg or draping her head
along her back, she's
too exact and sinuous
to convince an audience
she's serious. The natural elect,
they think, would be less pink,
less able to relax their necks,
less flamboyant in general.
They privately expect that it's some
poorly jointed bland grey animal
with mitts for hands
whom God protects.

THIS LIFE

It's a pickle, this life.
Even shut down to a trickle
it carries every kind of particle
that causes strife on a grander scale:
to be miniature is to be swallowed
by a miniature whale. Zeno knew
the law that we know: no matter
how carefully diminished, a race
can only be *half* finished with success;
then comes the endless halving of the rest—
the ribbon's stalled approach, the helpless
red-faced urgings of the coach.

Emptiness

Emptiness cannot be
compressed. Nor can it
fight abuse. Nor is there
an endless West hosting
elk, antelope, and the
tough cayuse. This is
true also of the mind:
it can get used.

VACATION

It would be pleasant to walk
in Stonehenge or other places
that have rocks arranged on the
basis of a plan, or plans,
inscrutable to modern man;
to wander among grinders
sunk deep in sheep pastures
or simply set on top Peruvian grit;
to gaze up at incisors
no conceivable jaw could fit;
to stretch to be ignorant enough,
scoured to a clean vessel
as pure as the puzzle, vestal
to a mystery involving people,
but without the heat of people.

No Rest for the Idle

The idle are shackled
to their oars. The waters
of idleness are borderless
of course and must always
be plied. Relief is foreign
on this wide and featureless
ocean. There are no details:
no shores, no tides, no times
when things lift up and then
subside, no sails or smokestacks,
no gravel gathered up and spit back,
no plangencies, no seabirds startled;
the weather, without the Matthew Arnold.

GLASS SLIPPERS

Despite the hard luck
of the ugly stepsisters,
most people's feet will fit
into glass slippers.
The arch rises, the heel
tapers, the toes align
in descending order
and the whole thing slides
without talcum powder
into the test slipper.
We *can* shape to the
dreams of another; we are
eager to yield. It is a
mutual pleasure to the holder
of the slipper and to the
foot held. It is a singular
moment—tender, improbable,
and as yet unclouded by the
problems that hobble the pair
when they discover that
the matching slipper

isn't anywhere, nor does
the bare foot even share
the shape of the other.
When they compare,
the slippered foot makes
the other odder: it looks
like a hoof. So many miracles
don't start far back enough.

WHEN FISHING FAILS

*"Your husband is very lucky," observed Smithers, "to have
ornithology to fall back upon when fishing fails."*
                    Cyril Hare, *Death Is No Sportsman*

When fishing fails, when no bait avails,
and nothing speaks in liquid hints
of where the fishes went for weeks,
and dimpled ponds and silver creeks
go flat and tarnish, it's nice if
you can finish up your sandwich,
pack your thermos, and ford
this small hiatus toward
a second mild and absorbing purpose.

So Different

A tree is lightly connected
to its blossoms.
For a tree it is
a pleasant sensation
to be stripped
of what's white and winsome.
If a big wind comes,
any nascent interest in fruit
scatters. This is so different
from humans, for whom
what is un-set matters
so oddly—as though
only what is lost held possibility.

HALF A LOAF

The whole loaf's loft
is halved in profile,
like the standing side
of a bombed cathedral.

The cut face
of half a loaf
puckers a little.

The bread cells
are open and brittle
like touching coral.

It is nothing like the middle
of an uncut loaf,
nothing like a conceptual half
which stays moist.

I say do not adjust to half
unless you must.

SPRING

Winter, like a set opinion,
is routed. What gets it out?
The imposition of some external season
or some internal doubt?
I see the yellow maculations spread
across bleak hills of what I said
I'd always think; a stippling of white
upon the grey; a pink the shade
of what I said I'd never say.

IMPERSONAL

The working kabbalist
resists the lure of
the personal. She
suspends interest
in the biblical list
of interdicted shellfish,
say, in order to
read the text another way.
It might seem to some
superficial to convert
letters to numerals
or in general refuse plot
in favor of dots or half circles;
it might easily seem
comical, how she
ignores an obviously
erotic tale except for
every third word,
rising for her like braille
for something vivid
as only the impersonal

can be—a crescent
bright as the moon,
a glimpse of a symmetry,
a message so vast
in its passage that
she must be utterly open
to an alien idea of person.

I MARVELED AT HOW GENERALLY I WAS AIDED

The Autobiography of Charles Darwin

I marvel at how generally
I am aided, how frequently
the availability of help
is demonstrated. I've had
unbridgeable distances collapse
and opposite objects coalesce
enough to think duress itself
may be a prayer. Perhaps not chance,
but need, selects; and desperation
works upon giraffes until their necks
can reach the necessary branch.
If so, help alters; makes seven vertebrae
go farther in the living generation;
help coming to us, not from the fathers,
not to the children.

FORCE

Nothing forced works.
The Gordian knot just worsens
if it's jerked at by a person.
One of the main stations
of the cross is patience.
Another, of course, is impatience.
There is such a thing as
too much tolerance
for unpleasant situations,
a time when the gentle
teasing out of threads
ceases to be pleasing
to a woman born for conquest.
Instead she must assault
the knot or alp or everest
with something sharp
and take upon herself
the moral warp of sudden progress.

MINERS' CANARIES

It isn't arbitrary;
it isn't curious;
miners' canaries
serve ordinary purposes
with just a fillip of
extra irony.
Something is always
testing the edges
of the breathable—
not so sweet, not so yellow,
but something is always
living at the wrong edge
of the arable; something
is always excused first
from the water table,
chalking the boundary
of the possible
from the far side;
even in the individual.

THE HINGE OF SPRING

The jackrabbit is a mild herbivore
grazing the desert floor,
quietly abridging spring,
eating the color off everything
rampant-height or lower.

Rabbits are one of the things
coyotes are for. One quick scream,
a few quick thumps,
and a whole little area
shoots up blue and orange clumps.

Deer

To lure a single swivel ear,
one tentative twig of a leg,
or a nervous tail here,
is to mark this place
as the emperor's park,
rife, I say rife, with deer.
For if one leaf against the littered floor
be cleft with the true arc,
all this lost ground, and more,
becomes a park. Everywhere
the nearest deer signals the nearest dark.
A buck looks up: the touch of his rack
against wet bark whispers a syllable
singular to deer; the next one hears
and shifts; the next head stops
and lifts; deeper and deeper into the park

POETRY IS A KIND OF MONEY

Poetry is a kind of money
whose value depends upon reserves.
It's not the paper it's written on
or its self-announced denomination,
but the bullion, sweated from the earth
and hidden, which preserves its worth.
Nobody knows how this works,
and how can it? Why does something
stacked in some secret bank or cabinet,
some miser's trove, far back, lambent,
and gloated over by its golem, make us
so solemnly convinced of the transaction
when Mandelstam says *gold*, even
in translation?

MASTERWORKS OF MING

Ming, Ming,
such a lovely
thing blue
and white

bowls and
basins glow
in museum
light

they would
be lovely
filled with
rice or
water

so nice
adjunct
to dinner

or washing
a daughter

a small
daughter
of course
since it's
a small basin

first you
would put
one then

the other
end in.

PAIRED THINGS

Who, who had only seen wings,
could extrapolate the
skinny sticks of things
birds use for land,
the backward way they bend,
the silly way they stand?
And who, only studying
bird tracks in the sand,
could think those little forks
had decamped on the wind?
So many paired things seem odd.
Who ever would have dreamed
the broad winged raven of despair
would quit the air and go
bandy-legged upon the ground,
a common crow?

OSPREY

The great taloned osprey
nests in Scotland.
Her nest's the biggest
thing around, a spiked basket
with hungry ugly osprey offspring
in it. For months she sits on it.
He fishes, riding four-pound salmon
home like rockets. They get
all the way there before they die,
so muscular and brilliant
swimming through the sky.

TURTLE

Who would be a turtle who could help it?
A barely mobile hard roll, a four-oared helmet,
she can ill afford the chances she must take
in rowing toward the grasses that she eats.
Her track is graceless, like dragging
a packing case places, and almost any slope
defeats her modest hopes. Even being practical,
she's often stuck up to the axle on her way
to something edible. With everything optimal,
she skirts the ditch which would convert
her shell into a serving dish. She lives
below luck-level, never imagining some lottery
will change her load of pottery to wings.
Her only levity is patience,
the sport of truly chastened things.

from *Elephant Rocks* (1996)

LIVING WITH STRIPES

In tigers, zebras,
and other striped creatures,
any casual posture
plays one beautiful set of lines
against another:
herringbones and arrows
appear and disappear;
chevrons widen and narrow.
Miniature themes and counterpoints
occur in the flexing and extending
of the smaller joints.
How can they stand to drink,
when lapping further complicates
the way the water duplicates their lines?
Knowing how their heads will zigzag out,
I wonder if they dread to start sometimes.

DOUBT

A chick has just so much time
to chip its way out, just so much
egg energy to apply to the weakest spot
or whatever spot it started at.
It can't afford doubt. Who can?
Doubt uses albumen
at twice the rate of work.
One backward look by any of us
can cost what it cost Orpheus.
Neither may you answer
the stranger's knock;
you know it is the Person from Porlock
who eats dreams for dinner,
his napkin stained the most delicate colors.

MIRAGE OASES

First among places
susceptible to trespass
are mirage oases

whose graduated pools
and shaded grasses, palms,
and speckled fishes give
before the lightest pressure
and are wrecked.

For they live
only in the kingdom
of suspended wishes,

thrive only at our pleasure
checked.

CHEMISTRY

Words especially
are subject to
the chemistry
of death: it is
an acid bath
which dissolves
or doubles
their strength.
Sentiments
which pleased
drift down
as sediment;
iron trees
grow from filament.

DEW

As neatly as peas
in their green canoe,
as discretely as beads
strung in a row,
sit drops of dew
along a blade of grass.
But unattached and
subject to their weight,
they slip if they accumulate.
Down the green tongue
out of the morning sun
into the general damp,
they're gone.

CRIB

From the Greek for
woven or *plaited*,
which quickly translated
to *basket*. Whence the verb
crib, which meant "to filch"
under cover of wicker
anything—some liquor,
a cutlet.
For we want to make off
with things that are not
our own. There is a pleasure
theft brings, a vitality
to the home.
Cribbed objects or answers
keep their guilty shimmer
forever, have you noticed?
Yet religions downplay this.
Note, for instance, in our
annual rehearsals of innocence,
the substitution of *manger* for *crib*—
as if we ever deserved that baby,
or thought we did.

BESTIARY

A bestiary catalogs
bests. The mediocres
both higher and lower
are suppressed in favor
of the singularly savage
or clever, the spectacularly
pincered, the archest
of the arch deceivers
who press their advantage
without quarter even after
they've won, as of course they would.
Best is not to be confused with *good*—
a different creature altogether,
and treated of in the goodiary—
a text alas lost now for centuries.

How Birds Sing

One is not taxed;
one need not practice;
one simply tips
the throat back
over the spine axis
and asserts the chest.
The wings and the rest
compress a musical
squeeze which floats
a series of notes
upon the breeze.

If the Moon Happened Once

If the moon happened *once*,
it wouldn't matter much,
would it?

One evening's ticket
punched with a
round or a crescent.

You could like it
or not like it,
as you chose.

It couldn't alter
every time it rose;

it couldn't do those
things with scarves
it does.

New Clothes

The emperor who
was tricked by the tailors
is familiar to you.

But the tailors
keep on changing
what they do
to make money.

(*Tailor* means
to make something
fit somebody.)

Be guaranteed
that they will discover
your pride.

You will cast aside
something you cherish
when the tailors whisper,
"*Only you could wear this.*"

It is almost never clothes
such as the emperor bought

but it is always something close
to something you've got.

CRUSTACEAN ISLAND

There could be an island paradise
where crustaceans prevail.
Click, click, go the lobsters
with their china mitts and
articulated tails.
It would not be sad like whales
with their immense and patient sieving
and the sobering modesty
of their general way of living.
It would be an island blessed
with only cold-blooded residents
and no human angle.
It would echo with a thousand castanets
and no flamencos.

LES PETITES CONFITURES

(The Little Jams)

These three pieces
in Satie's elegant notation
were just discovered
at the Métro station
where he rolled them
in a *Figaro* of April twenty-second,
nineteen twenty-seven,
and put them in a pipe
two inches in diameter, the type
then commonly used for banisters.
They are three sticky pieces
for piano or banjo—
each instrument to be played
so as to sound like the other.
That is really the hub
of the amusement. Each piece
lasts about a minute.
When they were first tried
after being in the pipe,
they kept rolling back up.
Really, keeping them flat
was half the banjo-piano
man's work.

Why Isn't It All More Marked

Why isn't it all
more marked,
why isn't every wall
graffitied, every park tree
stripped like the
stark limbs
in the house of
the chimpanzees?
Why is there bark
left? Why do people
cling to their
shortening shrifts
like rafts? So
silent.
Not why people *are*;
why not *more* violent?
We must be
so absorbent.
We must be
almost crystals,

almost all some
neutralizing chemical
that really does
clarify and bring peace,
take black sorrow
and make surcease.

LEARNING

Whatever must be learned
is always on the bottom,
as with the law of drawers
and the necessary item.
It isn't pleasant,
whatever they tell children,
to turn out on the floor
the folded things in them.

AGE

As some people age
they kinden.
The apertures
of their eyes widen.
I do not think they weaken;
I think something weak strengthens
until they are more and more it,
like letting in heaven.
But other people are
mussels or clams, frightened.
Steam or knife blades mean open.
They hear heaven, they think boiled or broken.

COUNSEL

It is possible
that even the best counsel
cannot be processed
by the body.
All supplements to
our personal chemistry
are screened by tiny
fanatical secret organs
that refuse much more than
they accept. It is hard
to add even minerals.
Iron tablets, for example,
are not correct
and pass through us like
windowless alien crafts.
What the body wants is so exact.

SILENCE

Silence is not snow.
It cannot grow
deeper. A thousand years
of it are thinner
than paper. So
we must have it
all wrong
when we feel trapped
like mastodons.

A Cat/A Future

A cat can draw
the blinds
behind her eyes
whenever she
decides. Nothing
alters in the stare
itself but she's
not there. Likewise
a future can occlude:
still sitting there,
doing nothing rude.

HOPE

What's the use
of something
as unstable
and diffuse as hope—
the almost-twin
of making do,
the isotope
of going on:
what isn't in
the envelope
just before
it isn't:
the always tabled
righting of the present.

LOSSES

Most losses add something—
a new socket or silence,
a gap in a personal
archipelago of islands.

We have that difference
to visit—itself
a going-on of sorts.

But there are other losses
so far beyond report
that they leave holes
in holes only

like the ends of the
long and lonely lives
of castaways
thought dead but not.

THE CABINET OF CURIOSITIES

It's hard for
minor monsters
born with more
of one thing
than others—
the curse of
double vision
in a single head,
or double ears.
If they are people
their careers
are always troubled—
self-accused,
God-hobbled—
the spilling cup
they took for a blessing—
their lives spent
mopping up,
apologizing.

HER POLITENESS

It's her politeness
one loathes: how she
isn't insistent, how
she won't impose, how
nothing's so urgent
it won't wait. Like
a meek guest you tolerate
she goes her way—the muse
you'd have leap at your throat,
you'd spring to obey.

Swept Up Whole

You aren't *swept up whole*,
however it feels. You're
atomized. The wind passes.
You recongeal. It's
a surprise.

ANY MORNING

Any morning
can turn molten
without warning.
Every object
can grow fluent.
Suddenly the kitchen
has a sulfur river
through it;
there is a burping
from the closet,
a release of
caustic gases
from the
orange juice glasses.
The large appliances
are bonding in a way
that isn't pleasant
on linoleum as friable
as bacon. We never
fathom how we caused it,
or why we
never see it coming
like Hawaii.

RELIEF

We know it is close
to something lofty.
Simply getting over being sick
or finding lost property
has in it the leap,
the purge, the quick humility
of witnessing a birth—
how love seeps up
and retakes the earth.
There is a dreamy
wading feeling to your walk
inside the current
of restored riches,
clocks set back,
disasters averted.

A Plain Ordinary
Steel Needle Can Float
on Pure Water

Ripley's Believe It or Not

Who hasn't seen
a plain ordinary
steel needle float serene
on water as if lying on a pillow?
The water cuddles up like Jell-O.
It's a treat to see water
so rubbery, a needle
so peaceful, the point encased
in the tenderest dimple.
It seems so *simple*
when things or people
have modified each other's qualities
somewhat;
we almost forget the oddity
of that.

DISTANCE

The texts
are insistent:
it takes two points
to make a distance.

The cubit,
for instance,
is nothing
till you use it.

Then it is rigid
and bracelike;
it has actual strength.

Something metal
runs through
every length—

the very armature
of love, perhaps.

Only distance
lets distance collapse.

WOODEN

In the presence of supple
goodness, some people
grow less flexible,
experiencing a woodenness
they wouldn't have thought possible.
It is as strange and paradoxical
as the combined suffering
of Pinocchio and Geppetto
if Pinocchio had turned and said,
I can't be human after all.

HEAT

There is a heat
coming off
anything we meet
our-sized and
mildly round.
Who has not found
herself warmed
by certain stones,
for example, or
made occasional
"mistakes" about things
that didn't turn out
to be people?
Perhaps we
share a shape
that loves itself,
a heat anterior
to life, further back
than hearts.
I postulate
a very early date
for when the warming
starts.

from *Say Uncle* (2000)

SAY UNCLE

Every day
you say,
*Just one
more try.*
Then another
irrecoverable
day slips by.
You will
say *ankle*,
you will
say *knuckle*;
why won't
you why
won't you
say *uncle*?

STAR BLOCK

There is no such thing
as *star block*.
We do not think of
locking out the light
of other galaxies.
It is light
so rinsed of impurities
(heat, for instance)
that it excites
no antibodies in us.
Yet people are
curiously soluble
in starlight.
Bathed in its
absence of insistence
their substance
loosens willingly,
their bright
designs dissolve.
Not proximity
but distance
burns us with love.

CORNERS

All but saints
and hermits
mean to paint
themselves
toward an exit

leaving a
pleasant ocean
of azure or jonquil
ending neatly
at the doorsill.

But sometimes
something happens:

a minor dislocation
by which the doors
and windows
undergo a
small rotation
to the left a little

—but repeatedly.
It isn't
obvious immediately.

Only toward evening
and from the
farthest corners
of the houses
of the painters

comes a chorus
of individual keening
as of kenneled dogs
someone is mistreating.

A Hundred Bolts of Satin

All you
have to lose
is one
connection
and the mind
uncouples
all the way back.
It seems
to have been
a train.
There seems
to have been
a track.
The things
that you
unpack
from the
abandoned cars
cannot sustain
life: a crate of
tractor axles,
for example,

a dozen dozen
clasp knives,
a hundred
bolts of satin—
perhaps you
specialized
more than
you imagined.

THE EXCLUDED ANIMALS

Only a certain
claque of beasts
is part of the
crèche racket

forming a
steamy-breathed
semicircle
around the
baby basket.

Anything more
exotic than
a camel
is out of luck
this season.

Not that the
excluded animals envy
the long-lashed
sycophants;

cormorants
don't toady,
nor do toads
adore anybody
for any reason.

Nor do the
unchosen alligators,
grinning their
three-foot grin
as they laze
in the blankety waters
like the blankets on Him.

MOCKINGBIRD

Nothing whole
is so bold,
we sense. Nothing
not cracked is
so exact and
of a piece. He's
the distempered
emperor of parts,
the king of patch,
the master of
pastiche, who so
hashes other birds'
laments, so minces
their capriccios, that
the dazzle of dispatch
displaces the originals.
As though brio
really does beat feeling,
the way two aces
beat three hearts
when it's cards
you're dealing.

BLANDEUR

If it please God,
let less happen.
Even out Earth's
rondure, flatten
Eiger, blanden
the Grand Canyon.
Make valleys
slightly higher,
widen fissures
to arable land,
remand your
terrible glaciers
and silence
their calving,
halving or doubling
all geographical features
toward the mean.
Unlean against our hearts.
Withdraw your grandeur
from these parts.

PATIENCE

Patience is
wider than one
once envisioned,
with ribbons
of rivers
and distant
ranges and
tasks undertaken
and finished
with modest
relish by
natives in their
native dress.
Who would
have guessed
it possible
that waiting
is sustainable—
a place with
its own harvests.
Or that in
time's fullness

the diamonds
of patience
couldn't be
distinguished
from the genuine
in brilliance
or hardness.

That Will to Divest

Action creates
a taste
for itself.
Meaning: once
you've swept
the shelves
of spoons
and plates
you kept
for guests,
it gets harder
not to also
simplify the larder,
not to dismiss
rooms, not to
divest yourself
of all the chairs
but one, not
to test what
singleness can bear,
once you've begun.

WINTER FEAR

Is it just winter
or is this worse.
Is this the year
when outer damp
obscures a deeper curse
that spring can't fix,
when gears that
turn the earth
won't shift the view,
when clouds won't lift
though all the skies
go blue.

GRAZING HORSES

Sometimes the
green pasture
of the mind
tilts abruptly.
The grazing horses
struggle crazily
for purchase
on the frictionless
nearly vertical
surface. Their
furniture-fine
legs buckle
on the incline,
unhorsed by slant
they weren't
designed to climb
and can't.

THE FOURTH WISE MAN

The fourth wise man
disliked travel. If
you walk, there's the
gravel. If you ride,
there's the camel's attitude.
He far preferred
to be inside in solitude
to contemplate the star
that had been getting
so much larger
and more *prolate* lately—
stretching vertically
(like the souls of martyrs)
toward the poles
(or like the yawns of babies).

HELP

Imagine *help*
as a syllable,
awkward but utterable.

How would it work
and in which distress?
How would one gauge
the level of duress
at which to pitch
the plea? How bad
would something
have to be?

It's hard,
coming from a planet
where if we needed something
we had it.

THE PIECES THAT FALL
TO EARTH

One could
almost wish
they wouldn't;
they are so
far apart,
so random.
One cannot
wait, cannot
abandon waiting.
The three or
four occasions
of their landing
never fade.
Should there
be more, there
will never be
enough to make
a pattern
that can equal
the commanding
way they matter.

DON'T LOOK BACK

This is not
a problem
for the neckless.
Fish cannot
recklessly
swivel their heads
to check
on their fry;
no one expects
this. They are
torpedoes of
disinterest,
compact capsules
that rely
on the odds
for survival,

unfollowed by
the exact and modest
number of goslings
the S-necked
goose is—
who if she
looks back
acknowledges losses
and if she does not
also loses.

It's Always Darkest Just Before the Dawn

But how dark
is *darkest*?
Does it get
jet—or tar—
black; does it
glint and increase
in hardness
or turn viscous?
Are there stages
of darkness
and chips
to match against
its increments,
holding them
up to our blindness,
estimating when
we'll have the
night behind us?

HERRING

A thousand
tiny silver
thoughtlets
play in the mind,
untarnished
as herring.

They shutter
like blinds,
then sliver,
then utterly
vanish.

Is it unkind
to hope
some will
eat others;
is it uncaring?

The Silence Islands

These are the
Silence Islands,
where what outsiders
would consider
nearly imperceptible
aural amusements
land like coconuts
on the crystalline
hammers and anvils
of the native inhabitants.
Theirs is a refinement
so exquisite that,
for example, to rhyme
anything with *hibiscus*
is interdicted anytime
children or anyone weakened
by sickness is expected.

CHESHIRE

It's not the cat,
it's the smile that
lasts, toothy
and ruthless.
It's facts like this
we like to resist—
how our parts
may lack allegiance
to the whole;
how the bonds
may be more casual
than we know; how
much of us
might vanish
and how well
some separate part
might manage.

YESES

Just behind
the door,
a second.
But smaller
by a few inches.
Behind which
a third again
diminishes.
Then more
and more,
forming a
foreshortened
corridor or
niche of yeses
ending in
a mouse's
entrance
with a knob
too small
to pinch.

CROWN

Too much rain
loosens trees.
In the hills giant oaks
fall upon their knees.
You can touch parts
you have no right to—
places only birds
should fly to.

AMONG ENGLISH VERBS

Among English verbs
to die is oddest in its
eagerness to be *dead*,
immodest in its
haste to be told—
a verb alchemical
in the head:
one speck of its gold
and a whole life's lead.

LIME LIGHT

One can't work
by lime light.

A bowlful
right at
one's elbow

produces no
more than
a baleful
glow against
the kitchen table.

The fruit purveyor's
whole unstable
pyramid

doesn't equal
what daylight did.

WHY WE MUST STRUGGLE

If we have not struggled
as hard as we can
at our strongest
how will we sense
the shape of our losses
or know what sustains
us longest or name
what change costs us,
saying how strange
it is that one sector
of the self can step in
for another in trouble,
how loss activates
a latent double, how
we can feed
as upon nectar
upon need?

DROPS IN THE BUCKET

At first
each drop
makes its
own pock
against the tin.
In time
there is a
thin lacquer
which is
layered and
relayered
till there's
a quantity
of water
with its
own skin
and sense
of purpose,
shocked at
each new violation
of its surface.

THE JOB

Imagine that
the job were
so delicate
that you could
seldom—almost
never—remember
it. Impossible
work, really.
Like placing
pebbles exactly
where they were
already. The
steadiness it
takes... and
to what end?
It's so easy
to forget again.

FAILURE

Like slime
inside a
stagnant tank

its green
deepening
from lime
to emerald

a dank
but less
ephemeral
efflorescence

than success
is in general.

FAILURE 2

There could be nutrients
in failure—
deep amendments
to the shallow soil
of wishes.
Think of the
dark and bitter
flavors of
black ales
and peasant loaves.
Think of licorices.
Think about
the tales of how
Indians put fishes
under corn plants.
Next time hope
relinquishes a form,
think about that.

MATRIGUPTA

of Ujjain, India, wrote a poem that so pleased Rajah
Vicrama Ditya HE WAS GIVEN THE ENTIRE STATE OF
KASHMIR. *The poet ruled Kashmir for five years (118–*
123) AND THEN ABDICATED TO BECOME A RECLUSE.
                                    Ripley's Believe It or Not

(What a Trojan horse)
thought Matrigupta,
rewarded for his verse
by Rajah Ditya
with one of the nicest
states in India.
(Why couldn't it
have been a gold watch
or an inscribed plate?
I'll never write again
at this rate.)

"I am too blessed,"
went the little thank-you
poem he had rehearsed,
but already his words
were getting reversed
and he said, "I am
blue tressed," which was
only the first indication
of how things were in Kashmir
before his abdication.

WATER UNDER THE BRIDGE

That's water under
the bridge, we say,
siding with the bridge
and no wonder,
given the sloping ways
of water which
grows so grey
and oily, toiling
slowly downward,
its wide dented
slide ever onward;
we aren't demented.

from *The Niagara River* (2005)

THE NIAGARA RIVER

As though
the river were
a floor, we position
our table and chairs
upon it, eat, and
have conversation.
As it moves along,
we notice—as
calmly as though
dining room paintings
were being replaced—
the changing scenes
along the shore. We
do know, we do
know this is the
Niagara River, but
it is hard to remember
what that means.

HOME TO ROOST

The chickens
are circling and
blotting out the
day. The sun is
bright, but the
chickens are in
the way. Yes,
the sky is dark
with chickens,
dense with them.
They turn and
then they turn
again. These
are the chickens
you let loose
one at a time
and small—
various breeds.
Now they have
come home
to roost—all
the same kind
at the same speed.

CARRYING A LADDER

We are always
really carrying
a ladder, but it's
invisible. We
only know
something's
the matter:
something precious
crashes; easy doors
prove impassable.
Or, in the body,
there's too much
swing or off-
center gravity.
And, in the mind,
a drunken capacity,
access to out-of-range
apples. As though
one had a way to climb
out of the damage
and apology.

SHARKS' TEETH

Everything contains some
silence. Noise gets
its zest from the
small shark's-tooth–
shaped fragments
of rest angled
in it. An hour
of city holds maybe
a minute of these
remnants of a time
when silence reigned,
compact and dangerous
as a shark. Sometimes
a bit of a tail
or fin can still
be sensed in parks.

WEAK FORCES

I enjoy an accumulating
faith in weak forces—
a weak faith, of course,
easily shaken, but also
easily regained—in what
starts to drift: all the
slow untrainings of the mind,
the sift left of resolve
sustained too long, the
strange internal shift
by which there's no knowing
if this is the road taken
or untaken. There are soft
affinities, possibly electrical;
lint-like congeries; moonlit
hints; asymmetrical pink
glowy spots that are not
the defeat of something,
I don't think.

The Elephant in the Room

It isn't so much
a complete elephant
as an elephant
sense—perhaps
pillar legs supporting
a looming mass,
beyond which it's
mostly a guess.
In any case, we
manage with relative
ease. There are just
places in the room
that we bounce off
when we come up
against; not something
we feel we have to
announce.

A Ball Rolls on a Point

The whole ball
of who we are
presses into
the green baize
at a single tiny
spot. An aural
track of crackle
betrays our passage
through the
fibrous jungle.
It's hot and
desperate. Insects
spring out of it.
The pressure is
intense, and the
sense that we've
lost proportion.
As though bringing
too much to bear
too locally were
our decision.

THE BEST OF IT

However carved up
or pared down we get,
we keep on making
the best of it as though
it doesn't matter that
our acre's down to
a square foot. As
though our garden
could be one bean
and we'd rejoice if
it flourishes, as
though one bean
could nourish us.

SHIPWRECK

I was shipwrecked beneath a stormless sky
in a sea shallow enough to stand up in.

Fernando Pessoa

They're laughable
when we get there—
the ultimate articulations
of despair: trapped
in a tub filling with
our own tears, strapped
to a breadstick mast
a mouse could chew
down, hopping around
the house in paper shackles
wrist and ankle. It's
always stagey. Being
lost is just one's fancy—
some cloth, some paste—
the essence of flimsy.
Therefore we
double don't know
why we don't take off
the Crusoe rags, step
off the island, bow
from the waist, accept
your kudos.

THE OTHER SHOE

Oh if it were
only the other
shoe hanging
in space before
joining its mate.
If the undropped
didn't congregate
with the undropped.
But nothing can
stop the midair
collusion of the
unpaired above us
acquiring density
and weight. We
feel it accumulate.

ATLAS

Extreme exertion
isolates a person
from help,
discovered Atlas.
Once a certain
shoulder-to-burden
ratio collapses,
there is so little
others can do:
they can't
lend a hand
with Brazil
and not stand
on Peru.

HE LIT A FIRE WITH ICICLES

For W.G. Sebald, 1944–2001

This was the work
of St. Sebolt, one
of his miracles:
he lit a fire with
icicles. He struck
them like a steel
to flint, did St.
Sebolt. It
makes sense
only at a certain
body heat. How
cold he had
to get to learn
that ice would
burn. How cold
he had to stay.
When he could
feel his feet
he had to
back away.

RATS' TAILS

For Joseph Brodsky, 1940–1996

All that's left of him is rats' tails.
There's a fate I could envy.
Joseph Brodsky

Let's say
some day
all that's
left of him
is rats' tails,
just scattered
bits of script:
a loose *e*,
an *s* or two,
a *g*, an almost–
n. If he had
hands he'd
rub them as
the test begins:
to see how little
will suggest
the rat again.

CHOP

The bird
walks down
the beach along
the glazed edge
the last wave
reached. His
each step makes
a perfect stamp—
smallish, but as
sharp as an
emperor's chop.
Stride, stride,
goes the emperor
down his wide
mirrored promenade
the sea bows
to repolish.

FELIX CROW

Crow school
is basic and
short as a rule—
just the rudiments
of *quid pro crow*
for most students.
Then each lives out
his unenlightened
span, adding his
bit of blight
to the collected
history of pushing out
the sweeter species;
briefly swaggering the
swagger of his
aggravating ancestors
down my street.
And every time
I like him
when we meet.

DESERT RESERVOIRS

They are beachless
basins, steep-edged
catches, unnatural
bodies of water wedged
into canyons, stranded
anti-mirages
unable to vanish
or moisten a landscape
of cactus adapted
to thrift, a wasteland
to creatures who chew
one another or grasses
for moisture. Nothing
here matches their gift.

EXPECTATIONS

We expect rain
to animate this
creek: these rocks
to harbor gurgles,
these pebbles to
creep downstream
a little, those leaves
to circle in the
eddy, the stains
and gloss of wet.
The bed is ready
but no rain yet.

IDEAL AUDIENCE

Not scattered legions,
not a dozen from
a single region
for whom accent
matters, not a seven-
member coven,
not five shirttail
cousins; just
one free citizen—
maybe not alive
now even—who
will know with
exquisite gloom
that only we two
ever found this room.

STARDUST

Stardust is
the hardest thing
to hold out for.
You must
make of yourself
a perfect plane—
something still
upon which
something settles—
something like
sugar grains on
something like
metal, but with
none of the chill.
It's hard to explain.

THINGS SHOULDN'T BE SO HARD

A life should leave
deep tracks:
ruts where she
went out and back
to get the mail
or move the hose
around the yard;
where she used to
stand before the sink,
a worn-out place;
beneath her hand
the china knobs
rubbed down to
white pastilles;
the switch she
used to feel for
in the dark
almost erased.
Her things should
keep her marks.
The passage
of a life should show;

it should abrade.
And when life stops,
a certain space—
however small—
should be left scarred
by the grand and
damaging parade.
Things shouldn't
be so hard.

The Past

Sometimes there's
suddenly no way
to get from
one part to
another, as though
the past were
a frozen lake
breaking up. But
not from the
top; not because
it's warmer
up here; it's not.
But from underneath
for some reason—
perhaps some heat
trapped on its own
for so long it's
developed seasons.

REVERSE DRAMA

Lightning, but not bright.
Thunder, but not loud.
Sometimes something
in the sky connects
to something in the ground
in ways we don't expect
and more or less miss except
through reverse drama:
things were heightened
and now they're calmer.

LEAST ACTION

Is it vision
or the lack
that brings me
back to the principle
of least action,
by which in one
branch of rabbinical
thought the world
might become the
Kingdom of Peace not
through the tumult
and destruction necessary
for a New Start but
by adjusting little parts
a little bit—turning
a cup a quarter inch
or scooting up a bench.
It imagines an
incremental resurrection,
a radiant body
puzzled out through

tinkering with the fit
of what's available.
As though what is is
right already but
askew. It is tempting
for any person who would
like to love what she
can do.

CHART

There is a big
figure, your age,
crawling, then
standing, now
beginning to bend
as he crosses
the stage. Or
she. A blurred
and generalized
projection of you
and me. For a
long time it seems
as remote
from the self
as the ape chart
where they rise up
and walk into man.
And then it seems
the realer part.

No Names

There are high places
that don't invite us,
sharp shapes, glacier
scraped faces, whole
ranges whose given names
slip off. Any such relation
as we try to make
refuses to take. Some
high lakes are not for us,
some slick escarpments.
I'm giddy with thinking
where thinking can't stick.

THIEVES

There are thieves
in the mind, their
dens in places
we'd prefer
not to know.
When a word
is lifted from
its spot, we show
no surprise,
replacing *supplies*
with *provender.*
Out here, it's
the tiniest stutter,
the subtlest patch—
an affordable loss
of no significance
whatever to the
plastic surface of
social commerce.
Should a bit vanish
from an event, we

likewise manage.
But back at the ranch,
a hoard is building.
The thieves are
hatching some
fantastic plot
made out of parts
we'd laugh to think
that they thought
matched.

LATE JUSTICE

Late justice may
be more useless
than none. Some
expungings or
making-rights
or getting-backs
lack the capacity
to correct. The
formerly aggrieved
become exacting
in unattractive
ways: intolerant
of delay, determined
to collect. And shocked—
shocked—at their
new unappeasableness,
who had so long
been so reasonable.

LIGHTHOUSE KEEPING

Seas pleat
winds keen
fogs deepen
ships lean no
doubt, and
the lighthouse
keeper keeps
a light for
those left out.
It is intimate
and remote both
for the keeper
and those afloat.

TUNE

Imagine a sea
of ultramarine
suspending a
million jellyfish
as soft as moons.
Imagine the
interlocking uninsistent
tunes of drifting things.
This is the deep machine
that powers the lamps
of dreams and accounts
for their bluish tint.
How can something
so grand and serene
vanish again and again
without a hint?

New Poems

ODD BLOCKS

Every Swiss-village
calendar instructs
as to how stone
gathers the landscape
around it, how
glacier-scattered
thousand-ton
monuments to
randomness become
fixed points in
finding home.
Order is always
starting over.
And why not
also in the self,
the odd blocks,
all lost and left,
become first facts
toward which later
a little town
looks back?

THE EDGES OF TIME

It is at the edges
that time thins.
Time which had been
dense and viscous
as amber suspending
intentions like bees
unseizes them. A
humming begins,
apparently coming
from stacks of
put-off things or
just in back. A
racket of claims now,
as time flattens. A
glittering fan of things
competing to happen,
brilliant and urgent
as fish when seas
retreat.

BAIT GOAT

There is a
distance where
magnets pull,
we feel, having
held them
back. Likewise
there is a
distance where
words attract.
Set one out
like a bait goat
and wait and
seven others
will approach.
But watch out:
roving packs can
pull your word
away. You
find your stake
yanked and some
rough bunch
to thank.

TRAIN-TRACK FIGURE

Imagine a
train-track figure
made of sliver
over sliver of
between-car
vision, each
slice too brief
to add detail
or deepen: that
could be a hat
if it's a person
if it's a person
if it's a person.
Just the same
scant information
timed to supplant
the same scant
information.

VIRGA

There are bands
in the sky where
what happens
matches prayers.
Clouds blacken
and inky rain
hatches the air
like angled writing,
the very transcription
of a pure command,
steady from a steady
hand. Drought
put to rout, visible
a mile above
for miles about.

DOGLEG

Birds' legs
do of course
all dogleg
giving them
that bounce.
But these are
not normal odds
around the house.
Only two of
the dog's legs
dogleg and
two of the cat's.
Fifty-fifty: that's
as bad as it
gets usually,
despite the
fear you feel
when life has
angled brutally.

LEDGE

Birds that love
high trees
and winds
and riding
flailing branches
hate ledges
as gripless
and narrow,
so that a tail
is not just
no advantage
but ridiculous,
mashed vertical
against the wall.
You will have
seen the way
a bird who falls
on skimpy places
lifts into the air
again in seconds—
a gift denied
the rest of us
when our portion
isn't generous.

THE PHARAOHS

The pharaohs killed those who had built the secret chambers
of the pyramids to ensure that any knowledge of their exis-
tence would be lost.
                Henning Mankell, *The White Lioness*

The moral is
simple: don't
help other people
with their secrets.
But within the
self, what defense
is there against
the pharaohs who
demand chambers
we must build
on pain of death
after which
we're killed?
A person is
as a kingdom
and can afford
some losses toward
the construction of
underground systems,
say the pharaohs,

shutting their
cunning doors
that never were
and won't be
evermore.

PENTIMENTI

"Pentimenti of an earlier position of the arm may be seen."
                                            Frick Museum

It's not simply
that the top image
wears off or
goes translucent;
things underneath
come back up,
having enjoyed the
advantages of rest.
That's the hardest
part to bear, how
the decided-against
fattens one layer down,
free of the tests
applied to final choices.
In this painting,
for instance, see how
a third arm—
long ago repented
by the artist—
is revealed,

working a flap
into the surface
through which
who knows what
exiled cat or
extra child
might steal.

BITTER PILL

A bitter pill
doesn't need
to be swallowed
to work. Just
reading your name
on the bottle
does the trick.
As though there
were some anti-
placebo effect.
As though the
self were eager
to be wrecked.

FINISH

The grape and plum
might be said to
tarnish when ripe,
developing some
sort of light dust
on their finish
which the least
touch disrupts.
It is this that
the great Dutch
still lifes catch,
the brush as much
in love with talc
as polish. Also
with the strange
seeing-in you notice
when a bruise mars
a fruit's surface.

EASTER ISLAND

*The people of the island built those amazing stone statues,
and in the process cut down every last tree. No trees, no
wood for houses and fires; no protection from erosion; no
useful species, and so on.*
Jon Carroll, *San Francisco Chronicle*

It worked without
a hitch: the last
big head rolled
down the last logs
to its niche.
As planned,
a long chorus
of monoliths
had replaced
the forest, staring
seaward, nicely
spaced, each with
a generous collar
of greensward,
and prepared to
stand so long
that it would be
a good trade: life,
for the thing made.

SPIDERWEB

From other
angles the
fibers look
fragile, but
not from the
spider's, always
hauling coarse
ropes, hitching
lines to the
best posts
possible. It's
heavy work
everyplace,
fighting sag,
winching up
give. It
isn't ever
delicate
to live.

Still Life with Lemons, Oranges and a Rose

(1663) Francisco de Zurbarán

Like two
giant's hands,
shade and
gravity collude
to squeeze away
the light and leave
the clay, rued
Zurbarán. Which
means he has to
find a counter way
to paint, unless he
wants his oranges
too to stick, glued
into a lump
like candy. And
now his wife
is sick.

MONK STYLE

In practice, it took 45 minutes to get his stride.
It was hard for Monk to play Monk.

National Public Radio

It may be
that Monk is
always playing
Monk but down
the hall. There are
long corridors
as in a school.
Monk must
approach himself,
join himself
at the bench and
sit awhile.
Then slip his
hands into his
hands Monk
style.

On the Nature of
Understanding

Say you hoped to
tame something
wild and stayed
calm and inched up
day by day. Or even
not tame it but
meet it half way.
Things went along.
You made progress,
understanding
it would be a
lengthy process,
sensing changes
in your hair and
nails. So it's
strange when it
attacks: you thought
you had a deal.

THE MAIN DIFFICULTY OF WATER WHEELS

was their inseparability from water.
Wikipedia

There are machines of
great generative power
that can only work locally
for one reason or another.
The great fixed wheels
moved by water
cannot be moved
from water. It hurts
to think of anything
wrenched out of where
it works. But not
just for the work.
Those buckets
drenching the river,
all the ornaments
of torque.

SPLITTING ICE

Like standing
on splitting ice
one foot on one
one on the
other piece.
Distressed like
the family of man
at the divorce
of the plates:
some cast into
a suddenly new
world as though
having sinned;
those kept behind
trapped and
bereft. But in
a *person*, one
foot will lift
and the split
resolve. So
why do the
self-saved
feel half left?

SHOOT THE MOON

To do it at all
we must do it
too soon: shoot
before the moon
to shoot the moon,
we learn, having
shot it dead,
bagged now and
heavy as a head.

More of the Same

More of the same
has a tell-tale
splice or hitch
after the first-of-
the-same (which,
at the time,
didn't go by that
name.) Things
are not quite
as fluid as we
wish, as though
there were
gaps in water,
bits of not-river;
and rivers were
a sequence of
patched fractures,
one discovered,
convincing by
speed alone like
life (ours now a
dropped dish.)

THE FIRST OF NEVER

Never dawns
as though
it were a day
and rises.

Our day-sense
says a day
can be out-waited.
So we wait.

That's the
only time
we've ever known:

it should be
getting late;
she should be
getting home.

Index of Titles